THE OFFICIAL TOTTENHAM HOTSPUR ANNUAL 2016

Written by Michael Bridge
Designed by Bradley Scott-Peterson

A Grange Publication

© [2015]. Published by Grange Communications Ltd., Edinburgh, under licence from Tottenham Hotspur Ltd. Printed in the EU.

Photographs © Action

ISBN 978-1-910199-55-

CONTENTS

Dear Supporters,

Welcome to the 2016 Official Tottenham Hotspur Annual.

We finished fifth in the Premier League last season, securing European football once again at White Hart Lane.

There were some memorable moments in 2015, particularly victories over London rivals Chelsea and Arsenal.

We also witnessed the emergence of Harry Kane. Harry scored an impressive 31 goals for Spurs, culminating in him winning the PFA Young Player of the Year award. Aside from Harry, it was a great year for the Academy as Nabil Bentaleb and Ryan Mason became established First Team regulars.

There is plenty to look forward to this year as our Head Coach Mauricio Pochettino continues to build an exciting squad. We're also well underway to delivering one of the best stadia in European football. We've already witnessed our worldwide support after trips to Malaysia, Australia, the United States and Germany in the last few months.

Thank you for your continued support.

Enjoy your new Annual.

Come on you Spurs!

Michael Bridge

BARCLAYS PREMIER LEAGUE REVIEW

Spurs guaranteed European football for the sixth successive season. There were plenty of memorable moments during the 2014/2015 Premier League season; great games, huge wins and new White Hart Lane heroes.

In Mauricio Pochettino's debut season as Head Coach, we witnessed several youngsters' introduction to the First Team. Harry Kane's rapid emergence became one of the biggest talking points in football. His dream season ended with the winning goal at Everton on the final day to pip Liverpool to a very respectable 5th position.

AUGUST

Pld: 3 W: 2 D: 0 L: 1   League table (as it stood): 6th

Spurs started the season with a difficult trip to London rivals, West Ham. The Hammers won all three meetings against us in the previous season. A fourth successive defeat was unthinkable. However, a Kyle Naughton red card, early in the first half, gave the home side the advantage. Mark Noble missed a penalty to keep it goalless. With the game heading towards a draw, Younes Kaboul found substitute Harry Kane, who played a clever through ball to debutant Eric Dier who hadn't stopped running from the back to pick up the ball and round Adrian to score a late winner. Our bright start to the season continued with a superb 4-0 win over QPR at White Hart Lane. Nacer Chadli put Spurs ahead before Eric Dier scored his second in successive matches when he powerfully met Erik Lamela's corner with a near post header. And it was 3-0 on 37 minutes with a truly wonderful goal.

We enjoyed a long period of possession – counted up as over two minutes long with 48 passes - which eventually led to Lamela turning his marker 40 yards from the goal. He advanced to the left-side of the area, before clipping over the perfect cross for Chadli to nod home his second of the game. Danny Rose found Emmanuel Adebayor to make it 4-0 in the second half and put Spurs top of the league at this very early stage of the season. The month ended in disappointment as Liverpool left the Lane with all three points after a 3-0 win.

We left the Stadium of Light frustrated after a late Harry Kane own goal earned a point for Sunderland. Nacer Chadli put Spurs ahead after two minutes, only for Adam Johnson to level 120 seconds later. Christian Eriksen put Spurs in front but we couldn't hold onto the lead. Chris Brunt's header made sure West Brom left White Hart Lane with all three points on a frustrating Sunday afternoon. Nacer Chadli's well-taken goal looked to have secured a memorable three points in the first north London derby of the season but Alex Oxlade-Chamberlain levelled for Arsenal.

OCTOBER   Pld: 3 W: 1 D: 0 L: 2
League table: 11th

Christian Eriksen's well-placed finish shortly before half-time, earned Spurs a 1-0 win over Southampton at White Hart Lane. Eriksen was on target again at Manchester City but it wasn't enough as the 2013/2014 champions were too strong, as Sergio Aguero scored all of City's four goals. The month ended in disappointment, as two second half Newcastle goals were enough to leave White Hart Lane with all three points. Emmanuel Adebayor put Spurs ahead in the first half.

November began with a 2-1 win over Aston Villa. It'll be remembered for Harry Kane's first of many League goals for the season. Spurs were a goal behind, but after Christian Benteke's red card we dominated and it was no surprise to see Nacer Chadli level. There was still time for Kane to score a stoppage time free-kick and send the away end into raptures.

Perhaps our most disappointing performance at White Hart Lane came against Stoke City.

Nacer Chadli pulled a goal back but Stoke ran out 2-1 winners. Our second stoppage time televised winner came at Hull, as Christian Eriksen scored a stunning winner from outside the box to earn all three points. Harry Kane levelled on 61 minutes. It was three successive televised victories after we beat Everton 2-1 at White Hart Lane. It was also the third successive occasion in the month where we came from behind to win, Eriksen and this time Roberto Soldado with our goals.

The month began with a disappointing 3-0 defeat to eventual champions Chelsea. Crystal Palace frustrated us at White Hart Lane three days later, leaving with a point after a goalless draw. Goals from Harry Kane and another late Christian Eriksen goal secured a 2-1 win at Swansea. Kane was on target again against Burnley at the Lane. Ashley Barnes levelled before an outstanding goal from Erik Lamela sealed victory for Spurs. We travelled

to newly-promoted Leicester on Boxing Day, and it was Kane and Eriksen again on target to earn a third successive win. An entertaining 0-0 draw against Manchester United at White Hart Lane left us well in contention for a European spot at the end of the year.

It was a New Year's Day to remember as we destroyed Chelsea at White Hart Lane. Diego Costa gave Chelsea the lead before Harry Kane scored, beating three Chelsea players to finish well past Thibaut Courtois. We went in front through Danny Rose and an Andros Townsend penalty in first half stoppage time put us 3-1 ahead. Kane, once again, got the better of John Terry and Gary Cahill to put Spurs 4-1 ahead. Eden Hazard pulled a goal back for Chelsea but Nacer Chadli made sure it was going to be a 'Glory Glory' night at the Lane. Terry scored late on but we held on to win 5-3 against Jose Mourinho's side. Kane-mania was spreading as his magnificent form continued. His next goal arrived at Crystal Palace. But it wasn't enough as Palace won 2-1, in Alan Pardew's first match in charge. Jermain Defoe returned to White Hart Lane as a Sunderland player in our next match. The former Spurs favourite was looking to retain his superb record of scoring on his debut at every club. Thankfully, that record came to an end as a John O'Shea own goal and yet another Eriksen effort, sealed a 2-1 win. Eriksen was on target again with a stunning free kick at West Brom. We added two more from Kane to earn a very impressive 3-0 win.

February started with a memorable win over north London rivals Arsenal. It was that man again Harry Kane, as we came from behind to earn the bragging rights. It was a superb performance full of character, desire and no shortage of quality. Kane was on target yet again at Anfield but a late Mario Balotelli goal earned a 3-2 win for Liverpool on a cold Tuesday night. Kane's 24th goal of the season arrived in

stoppage time against West Ham. It looked like our London neighbours were to leave White Hart Lane with all three points as they held a 2-0 lead with 10 minutes remaining but Danny Rose and Kane earned a point.

Just three days after a heart-breaking League Cup final defeat to Chelsea, the players deserved a lot of credit for this hard fought win over Swansea. Nacer Chadli opened the scoring with a well-taken volley. Ryan Mason added a second and a goal of the season contender from Andros Townsend, put Spurs 3-1 ahead. Ex-Spur Gylfi

Sigurdsson pulled a goal back for Swansea in the final minute. Two more goals from Harry Kane lifted Spurs back into the top six with a 2-1 win at QPR.

The most disappointing day in March was without doubt the 3-0 defeat to Manchester United. Kane's outstanding few months were rewarded with an England call-up. He celebrated this by scoring a hat-trick against Leicester City in a 4-3 win at White Hart Lane.

APRIL

Pld: 4 W: 1 D: 2 L: 1   League Table: 6th

Kane captained the side for the 0-0 draw at Burnley. A Christian Benteke goal then sealed a 1-0 win for Aston Villa at White Hart Lane. Nacer Chadli, Christian Eriksen and 30th goal of the season for Kane, earned a 3-1 win at Newcastle. Goals from Erik Lamela and Nacer Chadli helped Spurs secure a point in a tough encounter on Mauricio Pochettino's return to Southampton.

Sergio Aguero was the difference as Manchester City left north London with all three points. More disappointment followed with a 3-0 defeat at Stoke. But the season ended on a high note. Firstly, goals from Nacer Chadli and Danny Rose sealed a 2-0 win over Hull at White Hart Lane. Our final game of the season ended with PFA Young Player of the Year, Harry Kane scoring his 31st goal of a memorable campaign. That was enough to beat Everton and leapfrog Liverpool into fifth place and qualification into the Europa League group stages.

FINAL PREMIER LEAGUE TABLE

		P	W	D	L	F	A	GD	PTS
1	Chelsea	38	26	9	3	73	32	41	87
2	Manchester City	38	24	7	7	83	38	45	79
3	Arsenal	38	22	9	7	71	36	35	75
4	Manchester United	38	20	10	8	62	37	25	70
5	Tottenham Hotspur	38	19	7	12	58	53	5	64
6	Liverpool	38	18	8	12	52	48	4	62
7	Southampton	38	18	6	14	54	33	21	60
8	Swansea City	38	16	8	14	46	49	-3	56
9	Stoke City	38	15	9	14	48	45	3	54
10	Crystal Palace	38	13	9	16	47	51	-4	48
11	Everton	38	12	11	15	48	50	-2	47
12	West Ham United	38	12	11	15	44	47	-3	47
13	West Bromwich Albion	38	11	11	16	38	51	-13	44
14	Leicester City	38	11	8	19	46	55	-9	41
15	Newcastle United	38	10	9	19	40	63	-23	39
16	Sunderland	38	7	17	14	31	53	-22	38
17	Aston Villa	38	10	8	20	31	57	-26	38
18	Hull City	38	8	11	19	33	51	-18	35
19	Burnley	38	7	12	19	28	53	-25	33
20	Queens Park Rangers	38	8	6	24	42	73	-31	30

UEFA EUROPA LEAGUE REVIEW 2014/2015

The 2014/2015 Europa League campaign came to an end at the round of 32 stage after defeat at Fiorentina. With a huge League Cup final just three days away, Head Coach Mauricio Pochettino made several changes for the second leg in Italy. Despite the elimination, the campaign will be remembered for Harry Kane's superb form and a memorable stint in goal!

LIMASSOL 1-2 TOTTENHAM HOTSPUR

UEFA EUROPA LEAGUE *Play-off 1st leg*

This was the game where Harry Kane officially burst onto the First Team scene. Trailing 1-0, Roberto Soldado levelled on 74 minutes before Kane scored to put us in control of the tie.

TOTTENHAM HOTSPUR 3-0 LIMASSOL

Spurs won 5-1 on aggregate

UEFA EUROPA LEAGUE *Play-off 2nd leg*

Kane was on target again in the return leg as we guaranteed our place in the group stages. Goals from Paulinho and a penalty from Andros Townsend sealed a 5-1 win on aggregate.

PARTIZAN BELGRADE 0-0 TOTTENHAM HOTSPUR

UEFA EUROPA LEAGUE – *Group C*

Our Europa League Group C campaign started with a point in Belgrade with a hard-fought goalless draw against Partizan. Europa League winner Federico Fazio made his Spurs debut.

TOTTENHAM HOTSPUR 1-1 BESIKTAS

Harry Kane's stunning first half effort looked to be enough but an 89th minute penalty earned a point for the Turkish side.

TOTTENHAM HOTSPUR 5-1 ASTERAS TRIPOLIS

This was a night to remember at White Hart Lane. A true 'I was there' moment after Erik Lamela's incredible and audacious goal on 29 minutes, curling a 'Rabona' effort from 20 yards into the top corner of the Asteras net! Lamela added his second to cap a fantastic performance but that wasn't enough to secure the Man of the Match award as Harry Kane scored a superb hat-trick to seal a 5-1 win. If that wasn't enough drama, Kane ended the evening in goal after Hugo Lloris was dismissed in the 87th minute and we had used all our substitutes. He only had to face one shot, but unfortunately couldn't keep out Jeronimo Barrales' free-kick to give the visitors a consolation goal on the night.

ASTERAS TRIPOLIS 1-2 TOTTENHAM HOTSPUR

Harry Kane's excellent record in Europe continued with our second goal in Greece. Andros Townsend put Spurs ahead with a penalty as we edged closer to the round of 32.

TOTTENHAM HOTSPUR 1-0 PARTIZAN BELGRADE

Benji Stambouli's first goal for Spurs sealed victory at White Hart Lane. Academy graduate Harry Winks made his debut from the bench.

BESIKTAS 1-0 TOTTENHAM HOTSPUR

Cenk Tosun's second half goal consigned us to defeat and a runners-up spot on a frustrating night in Turkey, dominated by two floodlight failures.

FIRST LEG, TOTTENHAM HOTSPUR 1-1 FIORENTINA

EUROPA LEAGUE ROUND OF 32

Roberto Soldado's stunning effort put us in front but Jose Maria Basant's scrambled effort gave the Italian side a vital away goal.

SECOND LEG, FIORENTINA 2-0 TOTTENHAM HOTSPUR

(Fiorentina won 3-1 on aggregate)

Our European adventure came to an end in Florence where key moments in the match decided the tie. Roberto Soldado failed to take advantage of a golden opportunity when he broke clear with the game still all-square on 30 minutes. In the second half, Federico Fazio's pass was intercepted and Fiorentina broke away to score the opening goal through Mario Gomez. The Serie A side then secured their place in the last 16 when Mohamed Salah fired home the second on 71 minutes. Head Coach Mauricio Pochettino made a number of changes due to us having to face Chelsea at Wembley just three days later. A case of what might have been as we exited the competition.

CAPITAL ONE CUP REVIEW 2014/2015

"SPURS ARE ON THEIR WAY TO WEMBLEY" was the chant from supporters after a hard-fought aggregate victory over Sheffield United in the Capital One Cup semi-final. The competition saw Spurs play some of their best football of the season, culminating in an all-London Cup final against Chelsea.

3rd Round TOTTENHAM HOTSPUR 3-1 NOTTINGHAM FOREST

This is the game where Ryan Mason emerged in style. Trailing 1-0, Mauricio Pochettino introduced Mason and immediately made an impact, unleashing an unstoppable effort from some 35 yards. Roberto Soldado and Harry Kane made sure Spurs progressed to round four.

4th Round

TOTTENHAM HOTSPUR 2-0 BRIGHTON & HOVE ALBION

Erik Lamela's man-of-the-match performance helped Spurs reach the quarter-final. Spurs introduced Lamela as a second half substitute and he put the finishing touches to a well worked goal on 54 minutes. Harry Kane added a second to continue his good run in cup competitions.

5th Round

TOTTENHAM HOTSPUR 4-0 NEWCASTLE

One of the best performances of the season saw us beat Newcastle and reach the semi-finals. Nabil Bentaleb opened the scoring with a clever overhead kick from a corner. Nacer Chadli scored just 46 seconds into the second half and further goals from Harry Kane and Roberto Soldado set-up a semi-final tie with League One Sheffield United.

Semi-final 1st Leg

TOTTENHAM HOTSPUR 1-0 SHEFFIELD UNITED

Spurs went into this semi-final strong favourites, but Sheffield United's performances against Premier League sides in previous rounds, ensured we wouldn't take them lightly. It took a second half Andros Townsend penalty to earn a narrow lead, before a tricky second leg in Sheffield.

Semi-final 2nd Leg
SHEFFIELD UNITED 2-2 TOTTENHAM HOTSPUR

Spurs survived a huge scare to eventually reach the final. All looked to be going well after Christian Eriksen's free-kick. The Dane stepped up and hit a stunning right-foot effort up and over the wall and right into the top corner of the Blades' goal, a superb strike. Che Adams gave Sheffield United hope in the second half and set the Bramall Lane crowd alight when he scored his second, to level the tie on aggregate. From nowhere, Sheffield United looked to have the advantage, until Harry Kane collected the ball inside the United half with a long run, finding Eriksen and with his clever finish, put Spurs back in the lead on aggregate. Spurs held on, much to the delight of the brilliant 6,000 travelling support. A night of celebration – Spurs were back at Wembley.

Final
CHELSEA 2-0 TOTTENHAM HOTSPUR

Spurs arrived at Wembley looking to beat Chelsea for the second time in just three months. In a quiet first half, Chelsea went ahead shortly before half time through John Terry. Their second arrived early in the second half. Diego Costa's deflected effort eventually hitting the back of the net. The scoreline was harsh on Spurs, with both sides struggling to play their best football due to the heavy rain on the Wembley pitch. Chelsea were determined not to concede after the 5-3 defeat on January 1st and they did enough to lift the trophy, but we took plenty of positives away as this young Spurs squad experienced a major final.

FA CUP REVIEW

FA Cup 3rd Round

BURNLEY 1-1 TOTTENHAM HOTSPUR

Spurs received a difficult 3rd round tie. Nacer Chadli's second half goal looked to have been enough, but Sam Vokes levelled on 73 minutes to earn Burnley a replay.

FA Cup 3rd Round Replay

TOTTENHAM HOTSPUR 4-2 BURNLEY

Marvin Sordell and Ross Wallace gave Burnley a 2-0 lead but a much-changed Spurs side responded with goals from Paulinho, Etienne Capoue, Vlad Chiriches and Danny Rose to seal our place in the next round.

FA Cup 4th Round

TOTTENHAM HOTSPUR 1-2 LEICESTER

Our FA Cup run came to an end at home to Leicester City. Andros Townsend put Spurs ahead on 19 minutes, but Leonardo Ulloa levelled for Nigel Pearson's side. With seconds remaining, the tie looked to be heading for another replay, but Jeffrey Schlupp's shot somehow found its way past Michel Vorm to earn Leicester a dramatic win.

NABIL BENTALEB

It's fair to say Nabil Bentaleb's Spurs First Team debut was rather unexpected as Tim Sherwood decided to introduce the Academy product in December 2013. From the 50th minute, Bentaleb played a key role as Spurs beat Southampton 3-2 at St Mary's. Sherwood's preference of Bentaleb over senior members of the First Team raised eyebrows, but the Algerian international hasn't looked back since, establishing himself as a key member of the side. His first Spurs appearance is one he'll never forget.

"I have great memories. That's where my dreams started to come true. I can remember it like it was yesterday. Even warming-up was fantastic! Then I had the chance to go on, it went well, we won, perfect!"

Nabil joined us initially as a trialist in September 2011, signing Academy forms in January 2012, before making his debut at Southampton. He earned himself a place in Algeria's World Cup squad with his impressive performances. He, along with his teammates, received a heroic reception back home after reaching the second round of the competition.

Nabil made 35 appearances in all competitions in 2014/2015, forming a fine central midfield partnership with fellow Academy graduate Ryan Mason.

He opened his goalscoring account for us in the 4-0 win against Newcastle in the Capital One Cup in December, joined the Algeria squad again for the Africa Cup of Nations in January and, following his return, started every Premier League match until the end of the campaign. Nabil's performances were rewarded with a new five-year contract last summer.

Nabil briefly held the captain's armband after a number of substitutions on our post-season tour of Malaysia and Australia. Vocal on the pitch and one who thrives on the big stage – Bentaleb has all the qualities to become a future Spurs captain. Despite his rapid rise, Nabil believes the best is yet to come from him.

"You have to improve all the time and if you don't, I consider that a failure. That's how I see it. That is what has brought me to where I am now.
"The Club has given me their trust, I have to thank them for that and I'll keep working hard to achieve things with Spurs."

Harry Kane's incredible season naturally stole the spotlight, but Bentaleb's role in the Spurs midfield was a close second in helping the side secure fifth place in the Premier League. Kane's double won the north London derby at White Hart Lane but Bentaleb's performance made him a strong contender for the man-of-the-match award. Constantly breaking up play, Nabil made Spurs tick, creating the key assist for Kane's winner.

It's quite remarkable to think Nabil will have just celebrated his 21st birthday at the end of 2015, but his attitude and work ethic go way beyond his years.

"You can't become a champion in any sport without tasting defeat and disappointment along the way," he said. "That's a big thing for me.
"The great basketball player Michael Jordan said 'I scored 300 points, but I missed 600 to score 300'. It's a quote I always remember, so when you fall on the floor you get up and use the experience to make you stronger. That's what this squad will do."

Wise words from a player going from strength to strength.

At 23 years of age, you could forgive Ryan Mason if he thought his career would be best served away from White Hart Lane.

But such thoughts didn't enter his head. The midfielder embraced Mauricio Pochettino's clear message upon his arrival as Head Coach – every player had their chance to impress. After our pre-season tour of the United States, Mauricio said Mason's performance was one big plus point to come out of the trip to America. Despite his impressive pre-season, his big moment in a Spurs shirt didn't arrive until late September. Career-wise, it was life changing. Trailing Nottingham Forest 1-0 at White Hart Lane in the League Cup, Ryan picked up a pass from Ben Davies and unleashed an unstoppable effort into the top left-hand corner. Spurs went on to win the game 3-1. Three days later, Pochettino handed Mason his first start in the Premier League. Opponents – Arsenal in the north London derby. Ryan didn't look out of place and impressed many in the 1-1 draw at the Emirates. Since then, Mason has become a key fixture in the Spurs First Team, and now looks back on his early days at Spurs in a positive manner.

"I'm a big believer that everything happens for a reason and the time was right for me. Perhaps if I'd have played earlier in my career it might not have gone so well. I came on against Forest and it was meant to happen. It was a great feeling. It set me up and I kicked on from there."

Mason formed an impressive partnership with fellow Academy graduate Nabil Bentaleb. Both were instrumental in the 2-1 win over Arsenal at White Hart Lane. Mason's dream season got even better when he received a call-up to the England squad, replacing Adam Lallana for the Euro 2016 qualifier against Lithuania and a friendly in Italy. He made his England debut in Turin, replacing Jordan Henderson on 74 minutes. He made an immediate impact, an assist for Spurs teammate Andros Townsend. The celebration saw the Spurs quartet of Mason, Townsend, Harry Kane and Kyle Walker celebrating a goal for their national side. A proud moment for any Spurs fan.

Ryan went on to play 37 games in all competitions. Injury prevented him from adding to his one England cap last season. After a dream season, he thanked his Head Coach for the faith shown in him with Mason determined to stay at the Club he loves.

"I had opportunities to leave the Club but never wanted to because I always thought, imagined and dreamed I'd play for Spurs at White Hart Lane. I never felt that I'd want to leave and actually go through with it. There were times when I thought it might not happen, of course, but there was always something in the back of my head telling me that I would walk out at White Hart Lane one day."

And his head was right as he is now an established member of the Spurs midfield and an England international.

MAURICIO POCHETTINO

Mauricio enjoyed a highly successful playing career, making his debut in 1988 with Argentinian side Newell's Old Boys at the age of 16 and winning the Argentine Primera División with them in 1991. Two spells at Espanyol followed from 1994, sandwiched between time with Paris Saint-Germain and Bordeaux. He won two Copa del Rey titles with Espanyol and also earned 20 international caps with Argentina.

Espanyol was to be Pochettino's first managerial role. It was there where his high pressing attacking brand of football was first witnessed. With a lack of transfer funds, Pochettino promoted up to 20 players from the youth team. Espanyol finished 10th in Pochettino's first season, after taking over with the club in the bottom three. He left in 2012. By then, he had developed a reputation for an insistence on expansive attacking play. Pep Guardiola, coach of rivals Barcelona at the time, said he felt very close to Pochettino's style of football.

Mauricio became Southampton Manager in January 2013. At the time he spoke no English and many predicted he would struggle in an unforgiving league. However, victories over Manchester City, Liverpool and Chelsea made it clear Southampton had appointed someone special. Training sessions were intense and innovative. In the following season, Pochettino led Southampton to their highest-ever Premier League points tally and an eighth-place finish. His style of football was now fully ingrained in the squad. Academy players Luke Shaw and Adam Lallana were named in the PFA Team of the Year. Lallana and Shaw said they had developed significantly under Pochettino, prior to their high profile transfers to Liverpool and Manchester United respectively. Rickie Lambert, at 32, was on the plane to Brazil for the World Cup. In an interview, Lambert said Pochettino's coaching was the reason for his inclusion.

Mauricio resigned at Southampton to become the new Spurs Head Coach in May 2014. After his appointment, many expected his first season to be one of transition. But under his leadership there were many memorable moments in his first campaign at White Hart Lane. Reaching a Cup final, victory over Arsenal in the north London derby and

a comprehensive victory over Chelsea were the highlights. But his promotion of Harry Kane to first choice striker signalled his faith in the Academy. Kane repaid Pochettino's faith in style, scoring 31 goals in an incredible season.

Pochettino's faith in the Academy graduates paid dividends for Kane, Nabil Bentaleb, Ryan Mason, Andros Townsend and Danny Rose.

"Now it's easy to speak about Harry, but the process with the younger players is always important, to be careful, to build the future every day, step by step, not to jump 10 steps in one go."

During his first season, Pochettino assessed the squad he inherited. His preference for a high-pressure system resulted in some signings from previous regimes no longer being selected. The likes of Kane, Bentaleb and Mason were given their opportunities and never looked back. Pochettino now has a settled squad, a good mix of Academy and experience, and one he can rely on.

PLAYER PROFILES

HUGO LLORIS

The France captain Hugo Lloris is now in his fourth season at the Club. Hugo captained Spurs for the majority of last season and is considered a key member of the side. He is regarded as one of the best goalkeepers in the world.

MICHEL VORM

Dutch international goalkeeper Michel Vorm joined Spurs from Swansea in the summer of 2014. Michel made 14 appearances last season for Spurs, heavily featuring in our League Cup campaign.

KIERAN TRIPPIER

Kieran joined Spurs from Burnley in the summer. Kieran played more minutes, delivered more crosses and created more chances than any other full backs under the age of 25 in Europe's top five leagues during the 2014/2015 season.

PLAYER PROFILES

KYLE WALKER

Now in his seventh season at the Club, the England international returned from serious injury to make 21 appearances for Spurs last season. Kyle wrote his name in Spurs folklore by belting home the winner against Arsenal at White Hart Lane in October 2011.

HEUNG-MIN SON

The South Korea international joined Spurs from Bayer Leverkusen in August. Son originally moved to Germany as a teenager and came through the ranks at Hamburger SV, scoring on his Bundesliga debut in October 2010 against 1. FC Köln.

A consistent goalscorer throughout his time in Germany, Son made a total of 87 appearances, scoring 29 times at BayArena.

The 23-year-old is also a regular at international level with 11 goals in his 44 appearances for South Korea to date, including scoring against Algeria at the 2014 World Cup Finals.

DEANDRE YEDLIN

DeAndre's lightning pace impressed Spurs during the 2014 World Cup. The right-back completed the 2014 MLS season with Seattle - making it into the MLS All Star team for the second time - before joining us in January 2015. Yedlin will be out on loan at Sunderland for 2015/2016.

PLAYER PROFILES

Jan is a key member of the First Team. The Belgium international often captained the side last season and has also held the armband for his national side. Jan is also very capable at left-back.

JAN VERTONGHEN

ERIC DIER

England Under-21 international joined Spurs from Sporting Lisbon in July 2014. Eric gained instant hero status with a last-minute winner at West Ham on his debut in August 2014! He followed up with a goal on his full home debut in the 4-0 win against QPR. The versatile defender is primarily a centre-back but is equally capable at right-back.

PLAYER PROFILES

FEDERICO FAZIO

Tall, commanding central defender joined us from Sevilla in August 2014. Capped twice for Argentina, Fazio went on to make 194 appearances for the La Liga side and was also a key member of their Europa League winning team two years ago, beating Benfica on penalties in the final in Turin.

BEN DAVIES

DANNY ROSE

Exciting young Welsh left-back joined Spurs in July 2014. Ben made 32 appearances for Spurs last season before his season was ended due to a dislocated shoulder. Ben was recently part of an impressive Wales side during a successful Euro 2016 qualifying campaign.

Danny enjoyed his best spell at Spurs during Mauricio Pochettino's first season at the Club. The flying left-back was called-up by England Head Coach Roy Hodgson but injury prevented him from winning his first cap.

PLAYER PROFILES

MOUSA DEMBELE

Mousa is now in his fourth season at White Hart Lane. The Belgium international made 40 appearances for Spurs last season. Dembele joined Spurs from Fulham in August 2012 and scored on his debut against Norwich.

RYAN MASON

Home-grown midfielder sparked his Spurs career in September 2014.

Almost six years after his First Team debut aged just 17 in 2008, Ryan scored his first senior goal in the Capital One Cup against Nottingham Forest before his Premier League debut in no less than the north London derby three days later.

Ryan joined our full-time Academy set-up in 2007 and made his First Team debut in the Europa League match against NEC Nijmegen in November 2008. He made his England debut in March 2015, creating the assist for Andros Townsend's equaliser.

PLAYER PROFILES

ALEX PRITCHARD

Alex enjoyed a highly successful loan spell at Brentford last season, winning their Players' Player of the Year award. The attacking midfielder made 45 league appearances for Brentford, scoring 12 goals, securing a place in the England U21 side for the European Championships.

NABIL BENTALEB

A successful product of the Spurs Academy, Nabil is now a key member of the Spurs side. The Algeria international featured in the 2014 World Cup. Nabil made 35 appearances for Spurs last season and briefly captained the side against Sydney FC on our post-season tour.

DELE ALLI

Dele signed for Spurs in January 2015 but was loaned back to MK Dons for the remainder of the season. Dele enjoyed an outstanding season with 16 goals in 39 appearances in League One as the Dons were promoted automatically into the Championship as runners-up behind Bristol City.

His performances were recognised with a place in the PFA's League One Team of the Season and he was voted the Football League's Young Player of the Season.

PLAYER PROFILES

Tom enjoyed a successful spell at Swansea last season. A clever midfielder with an impressive passing range, the England Under-21 international is looking to break into the Spurs First Team in 2016.

Lightning winger Andros Townsend is another Academy graduate to make an impressive transition to First Team football at Spurs. Andros is now a regular in the England squad and scored a brilliant goal against Italy in March 2015.

ANDROS TOWNSEND

NACER CHADLI

The Belgium international enjoyed an impressive second season at White Hart Lane, scoring 13 goals. Nacer is comfortable in any role behind the striker, but was used primarily on the lef hand side last season.

CLINTON NJIE

Cameroon international joined Spurs from Lyon in August 2015. Clinton can play as centre-forward or from either the left or right wing, Njie made his debut for Lyon in November 2012 against Reims and went on to represent them on 43 occasions in total. Njie also has a prolific record at international level with six goals in his 11 appearances to date for Cameroon.

HARRY KANE

After an incredible season, Harry won the PFA Young Player of the Year award. Harry is the first player since Gary Lineker to score over 30 goals in a single season for Spurs. His form led to an England call-up and he scored his first international goal against Lithuania, just seconds after being brought on as a substitute. Harry also captained Spurs against Burnley in April 2015.

PLAYER PROFILES

Central defender Kevin joined us from Koln in May, 2015. The 22-year-old moved to Germany in 2012 from LASK Linz in his native Austria. Kevin helped Koln earn promotion to the Bundesliga in 2014, and was a standout performer in their first season back in the top flight this year. He made 72 appearances in total during his time in Germany, scoring twice.

Erik joined Spurs from Roma in August 2013. A back injury restricted his playing time in his first season at the Club, Erik responded with 46 appearances out of 57 in all competitions in 2014/2015.

He scored five goals - including one of the moments of the season with his spectacular 'Rabona' goal against Asteras Tripolis in the Europa League.

EMMANUEL ADEBAYOR

Emmanuel is now in his fifth season at Spurs. The Togo international rarely featured last season, scoring twice in 10 games, but he has scored goals at every club he played for.

TOBY ALDERWEIRELD

Versatile defender Toby joined us from Atletico Madrid in July, 2015.

A Belgium international, he came through the ranks at Ajax, making 186 appearances and scoring 15 goals during nine years with the Eredivisie champions, where he lifted three league titles and one Dutch Cup.

Toby joined Spanish side Atletico in 2013 and was part of the squad that won the La Liga title on the last day of the season as well as reaching the Champions League final in the same year.

He made 22 appearances in all for Diego Simeone's side, scoring twice, before impressing on loan at Southampton last season.

CHRISTIAN ERIKSEN

Now in his third season at the Club, Christian is a key member of the Spurs side. After an impressive first season at the Club, the Denmark international scored 12 goals in 48 appearances last season, including dramatic late winners against Hull, Swansea, Leicester and Sunderland. Christian also scored twice at Sheffield United to help earn Spurs a place in the League Cup final.

DERBY DELIGHT

It's hard to decide on a favourite moment of 2015, so we've tried to help you with the best images from our 2-1 victory in the north London derby and our stunning 5-3 win over Chelsea.

It's easy to keep up-to-date with your favourite Spurs star. Follow them via their personal Twitter accounts.

Andros Townsend - @andros_townsend

Tom Carroll - @tom_carroll92

Harry Kane - @hkane28

Jan Vertonghen - @Jan_Vertonghen

Kyle Walker - @kylewalker2

Kieran Trippier - @trippier2

Kevin Wimmer - @kevin28wimmer

Dele Alli - @dele_alli36

Josh Onomah - @Joshuaonomah10

Harry Winks - @HarryWinks_

Eric Dier - @ericdier

Federico Fazio - @Fede2Fazio

DeAndre Yedlin - @yedlinny

Michel Vorm - @Vorm_Official

Ben Davies - @Ben_Davies33

Nabil Bentaleb - @nabilbentaleb42

Erik Lamela - @Coco_Lamela

Christian Eriksen - @ChrisEriksen8

Nacer Chadli - @NChadli

Alex Pritchard - @pritch_93

Ryan Mason - @Ryan_Mason13

Mousa Dembele - @mousadembele

Toby Alderweireld - @Alderweireldtob

MEET THE STAFF
Mauricio Pochettino's coaching team

MIGUEL D'AGOSTINO
First Team Coach

Born: 5 October 1971

Previous clubs: Al Ittihad, Espanyol, Southampton

Jesus followed Mauricio Pochettino to Spurs in May 2014 after a successful spell as Southampton Assistant Manager. Jesus also worked alongside our Head Coach at Espanyol as Fitness Coach. Born in Spain, Jesus has coached for 18 years at Al Ittihad, Almeria, Rayo Vallecano, Pontevedra, Real Murcia, Castellon and Tarragona.

Born: 01 January 1972

Previous clubs: Espanyol, Southampton

Miguel, like Jesus, followed Mauricio Pochettino to White Hart Lane from Southampton. He played alongside Pochettino for Argentinian side Newell's Old Boys in the early 1990s. After leaving his position as Chief Scout at French side Brest, he joined Pochettino's coaching staff at Espanyol.

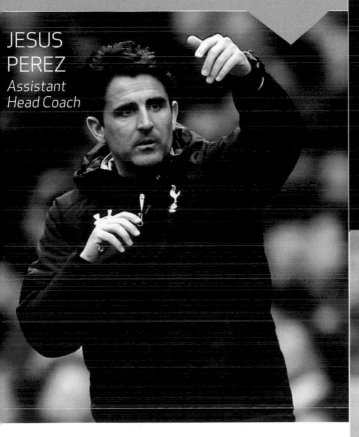

JESUS PEREZ
Assistant Head Coach

Born: 12 October 1970

Previous clubs: Espanyol, Southampton

The Club appointed Toni as Goalkeeping Coach in May 2014. After leaving Barcelona, he had a brief spell at Rayo Vallecano, before making over 200 appearances for Espanyol, where he met then team-mate Mauricio Pochettino. Toni won three caps for Spain and won a gold medal for Spain in the 1992 Olympics. He returned to Espanyol as Assistant Coach to Mauricio, before following him to Southampton.

INTERNATIONAL SPURS

International weekend on Hotspur Way can be a quiet time with many of the team away playing for their country. As you can see, Spurs have many international players, from all over the world.

Andros Townsend - England

Harry Kane - England

Hugo Lloris - France

Nabil Bentaleb - Algeria

Kyle Walker - England

Christian Eriksen - Denmark

DeAndre Yedlin - USA

Ryan Mason - England

Kevin Wimmer - Austria

Erik Lamela - Argentina

ic Dier - ngland

Mousa Dembele - Belgium

Jan Vertonghen - Belgium

Ben Davies - Wales

Nacer Chadli - Belgium

43

DO YOU WANT TO KNOW WHY
TOTTENHAM HOTSPUR IS SUCH A SPECIAL CLUB ??

Regardless of league positions, Spurs have always attracted world class talent. Some developed into White Hart Lane legends. In 2014, we profiled Jimmy Greaves, Jurgen Klinsmann, Dave Mackay, Ricky Villa and Pat Jennings. In 2015, we introduced Ossie Ardiles, Teddy Sheringham, Danny Blanchflower, Steve Perryman and Martin Chivers. Below are five more greats who have graced the White Hart Lane turf.

GARY LINEKER

Former England striker Gary Lineker scored 67 goals in 105 League games for Spurs and 80 in 138 in total. After a successful spell at Barcelona, Manager Terry Venables brought Gary back to England. He went on to become our top scorer in each of his three seasons at White Hart Lane. Two goals against Arsenal in the 1991 FA Cup semi-final will be fondly remembered by Spurs fans. Gary ended his playing career at Japanese side Grampus Eight and now enjoys presenting Match of the Day on the BBC and Champions League football on BT Sport.

ALAN MULLERY

Alan Mullery made 373 competitive appearances for Spurs after signing from Fulham. He replaced our double-winning captain Danny Blanchflower in midfield. Mullery was part of our 1967 FA Cup winning side, which coincided with a regular run in the England team and the 1970 World Cup. He took over the captaincy from Dave Mackay and led the side to the 1971 League Cup and the UEFA Cup in 1972. Today, Alan regularly appears on matchdays at White Hart Lane as one of our popular Club Legends. In 2015, Mullery was inducted into the National Football Museum's English Hall of Fame.

PAUL GASCOIGNE

One of the biggest characters English football has ever seen. 'Gazza' joined Spurs from Newcastle in 1988 for £2million. Big money back then... but in reality, Gascoigne was priceless. Unique is just one of a number of words used to describe a footballer who could do anything with the ball at his feet. His greatest moment in a Spurs shirt was his 30-yard free-kick in the 1991 FA Cup semi-final against Arsenal. It's a goal that is still shown around the world and one that will always live long in the memory of any Spurs fan, young or old. A serious knee injury in the final delayed his move to Lazio, but after his recovery, he went on to become a firm favourite in Rome and Glasgow Rangers. A natural genius loved by all in the football world.

CHRIS WADDLE

Chris Waddle was one of the most exciting wingers in English football. Chris spent over four years at White Hart Lane, and is considered a Spurs legend. Chris famously worked in a sausage factory while playing non-league football, before Newcastle United signed him in 1980. His partnership with Glenn Hoddle was the envy of teams across the country. After recovering from long-term injuries, Waddle returned to score a number of stunning goals, including a 35-yard chip at Southampton. Marseille paid £4.5m for his services in 1989 - at that time, Waddle was the third most expensive player in the world behind Maradona and Ruud Gullit

RAY CLEMENCE

After saying goodbye to, arguably, the best goalkeeper to have graced the White Hart Lane turf, Pat Jennings, the Spurs supporters didn't have to wait too long for the next top class number one. Ray won virtually every honour during his time at Liverpool, but he arrived at Spurs with just as much hunger and desire. He made over 300 appearances for the Club, collecting an FA Cup winners' medal in 1981/1982. Ray became assistant manager to Doug Livermore in the 1992/1993 Season and is still a regular visitor to White Hart Lane.

GOAL OF THE SEASON

RYAN MASON VS NOTTINGHAM FOREST

Thousands of you took time to vote both on tottenhamhotspur.com and via @SpursOfficial on Twitter. Here are the top 10.

ERIC DIER VS WEST HAM   NACER CHADLI VS STOK

Ben Davies popped the ball inside to substitute Ryan Mason who took a touch and unleashed a superb 25-yard drive right into the top corner.

With time running out Younes Kaboul pinged a pass into Harry Kane, he picked out Eric Dier's run across the back line from right to left and through on goal, the England Under-21 international picked up the ball, skipped past Adrian and slotted home.

Danny Rose delivered a deep cross from the left and it fell perfectly for Nacer Chadli to lash home on the volley

HARRY KANE VS ARSENAL

CHRISTIAN ERIKSEN VS SHEFFIELD UNITED

Nabil Bentaleb sent over a superb cross from the left channel, 30 yards out and Harry Kane rose to head the ball back across David Ospina's goal and into the far corner to give us the lead and eventually the victory.

From just outside of the penalty area on t right hand side, Christian Eriksen stepped and hit a stunning right-foot effort up and the wall and right into the top corner of th Blades' goal, a superb strike.

ERIK LAMELA vs BURNLEY

Jan Vertonghen sent Nacer Chadli away down the left, and the ball found its way across the pitch to Erik Lamela via Harry Kane and Ryan Mason. The Argentine cut inside onto his left and sent a delightful curling effort past the despairing dive of Tom Heaton and into the far corner.

NACER CHADLI vs NEWCASTLE

Nacer Chadli shifted the ball onto his left foot to wrong-foot two Newcastle defenders, before dipping a shot from 25 yards past Tim Krul and into the bottom corner.

AND THE CLEAR WINNER IS...

Erik Lamela's famous 'rabona' against Asteras Tripolis was selected by supporters as our Under Armour Goal of the Season for 2014/2015. Meeting a loose ball 20 yards from goal in the Europa League group stage clash with the Greek side on 23 October 2014, Erik wrapped his left foot around his right and sent a curling effort into the top corner of the net to put us 2-0 up on the night.

UNDER ARMOUR GOAL OF THE SEASON 2014/2015

Erik Lamela, first goal vs Asteras Tripolis
(23 October 2014) – 37.1%

Harry Kane, second goal vs Arsenal
(7 February 2015) – 17.6%

Christian Eriksen, first goal vs Sheffield United
(28 January 2015) – 9.3%

Erik Lamela vs Burnley
(20 December 2014) – 9.2%

Nacer Chadli vs Stoke City
(9 November 2014) – 6.9%

Ryan Mason vs Nottingham Forest
(24 September 2014) – 5.3%

Andros Townsend vs Swansea City
(4 March 2015) – 4.4%

Eric Dier vs West Ham United
(16 August 2014) – 4.2%

Danny Rose vs Hull City
 (16 May 2015) – 3.9%

Nacer Chadli vs Newcastle United
(19 April 2015) – 2.1%

DANNY ROSE vs HULL

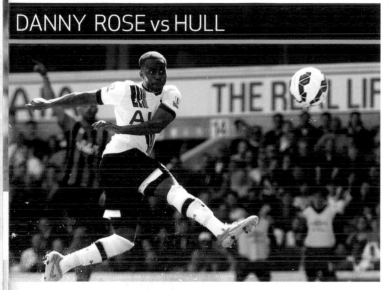

The ball came to Ryan Mason on the edge of the area, he dinked a ball over the top to find Danny Rose who sliced his volley from eight yards into the top right corner of Steve Harper's net.

ANDROS TOWNSEND vs SWANSEA

With the ball falling nicely for Andros Townsend in our own half, the England winger put the burners on as he roared forwards down the left and into the area, before cutting back onto his right and firing into the net.

QUIZ AND PUZZLE ANSWERS

P.53 GUESS THE GAME

1. 28 January 2015 -
   Sheffield United 2-2 Tottenham Hotspur

3. 1 January 2014 - Manchester United 1-2
   Tottenham Hotspur

2. 7 February 2015 -
   Tottenham Hotspur 2-1 Arsenal

4. 4 March 2007 -
   West Ham United 3-4 Tottenham Hotspur

P.37 WORDSEARCH

```
A  I  E  F  I  R  M  A  S  O  N  I  Y
X  H  D  E  V  J  M  N  L  N  T  S  R
N  T  U  S  O  N  O  I  A  A  G  E  E
W  A  L  K  E  R  N  M  S  S  B  L  O
G  N  B  N  R  S  Y  A  G  O  R  M  A
N  A  A  B  E  N  T  A  L  E  B  M  Y
C  K  D  A  R  Y  O  T  I  D  L  Q  A
A  L  L  I  B  H  Q  P  T  S  X  S  G
B  N  P  R  T  K  P  I  M  B  K  M  W
B  O  B  C  N  I  D  D  W  I  R  R  O
N  V  N  Y  R  O  S  E  S  T  I  A  G
E  W  R  T  B  C  L  K  E  S  G  T  E
Z  B  U  N  E  R  E  R  I  K  S  E  N
```

P.48 SUPER SPURS QUIZ

1. Manchester United
2. Erik Lamela
3. Cologne
4. Fiorentina
5. Real Madrid & AC Milan
6. 31
7. Nottingham Forest
8. 42
9. True
10. Eight
11. Kyle Walker, Ryan Mason, Andros Townsend, Harry Kane
12. Northumberland Park
13. Ledley King
14. Peter Crouch
15. FC Twente

P.53 GUESS THE PLAYER

1. Van der Vaart
2. Scott Parker
3. Eric Dier
4. Mido
5. Danny Rose
6. Michel Vorm

WHERE'S CHIRPY?